Learning English with the Bible

DIAGRAMMING GUIDE

BY
LOUISE M. EBNER

AMG
PUBLISHERS

ISBN 0-89957-602-8

Printed in the United States of America
01 00 99   9 8 7

Learning English with the Bible

DIAGRAMMING GUIDE

ENGLISH GRAMMAR DIAGRAMS
BASED ON THE BOOK OF JOSHUA

BY
LOUISE M. EBNER

JOHN 20:31

"BUT THESE ARE WRITTEN, THAT YE MIGHT BELIEVE THAT
JESUS IS THE CHRIST, THE SON OF GOD; AND THAT BELIEVING
YE MIGHT HAVE LIFE THROUGH HIS NAME."

TABLE OF CONTENTS

Sratis

121557

DIAGRAMS

● A *diagram* is a pictorial portrayal of a sentence. Many times grammatical concepts become clear to a student when a diagram is made.
Below are examples of diagrams of various sentence patterns.

I. Subject and Predicate — Pattern 1
Examples:

a. God rules.

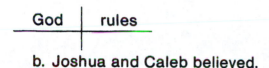

b. Joshua and Caleb believed.

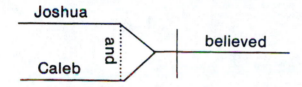

c. They went and returned.

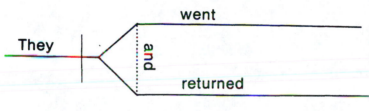

d. Go.

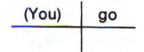

7

EXERCISE 1

Diagram the following sentences based on pattern 1.

1. Jesus lives.

2. Joshua led.

3. People were praying.

4. They yielded.

5. Men and women were working.

II. Modifiers

A. Now develop pattern 1 type of sentence by adding adjectives. Remember that adjectives modify nouns and pronouns.

Examples:

a. A great multitude followed.

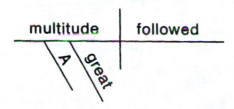

b. The seven priests and the armed men walked.

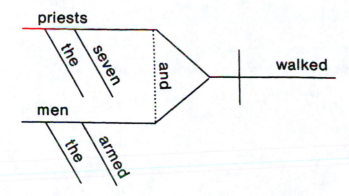

c. The strong and faithful man believed.

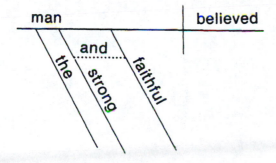

EXERCISE 2

Diagram the following sentences.

1. The twelve tribes will proceed.

2. The fortified city fell.

3. The healthy cattle and the spoils were surrendered.

4. An altar was built.

5. The young harlot and her family were delivered.

B. Continue developing pattern 1 type sentence by adding adverbs. Adverbs modify verbs, adjectives, and other adverbs.

Examples:

a. A very great multitude followed closely.

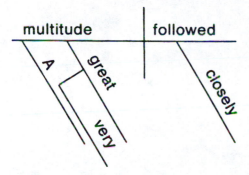

b. The old people and the young children walked slowly and carefully.

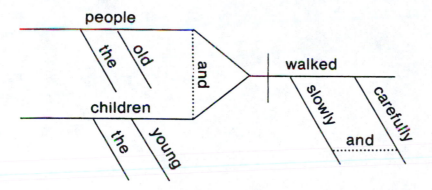

EXERCISE 3

Diagram the following sentences.

1. Jericho was straitly shut up.

2. Blow very loudly.

3. Do not steal.

4. The extremely clever spies went in and looked around.

5. An unknown visitor appeared.

C. Prepositional phrases can be added to pattern 1 sentences.

Examples:

a. Joshua fell on his face to the ground.

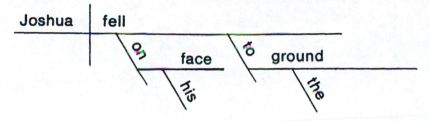

b. The children of Israel obeyed this time.

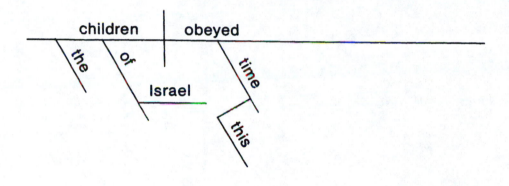

13

EXERCISE 4

Diagram the following sentences.

1. The people shouted with a loud voice.

2. The great walls fell to the ground.

3. The Lord was with Joshua.

4. The silver, gold, and vessels of brass and iron were not stolen by the people.

5. The fame of Joshua was raised throughout the land.

D. Appositives are placed next to the noun which they dentify.

   Example:

   Achan, the son of Carmi, transgressed.

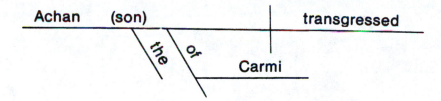

EXERCISE 5

Diagram the following sentences.

1. Jericho, the mighty city, fell to the army of Joshua.

2. Rahab, the harlot, was spared.

3. The Israelites fled before the men of Ai, a wicked group.

4. The covenant between God and man had been broken.

5. Joshua, an obedient man, and the priests prayed fervently.

E. Nouns of direct address and interjections are placed above the subject of the sentence.

Examples:

a. Sir, are you with us?

b. Yes, I am on your side.

EXERCISE 6

Diagram the following sentences.

1. Joshua, do not go to the people of Ai.

2. Well, his army proceeded to the east side of Bethel.

3. The army of the Israelites fled from the forces of Ai.

4. Lord, do you care about us?

5. Yes, an accursed thing is in the midst of thee.

III. Complements

A. *Direct object.* A direct object is a noun or pronoun which receives the action of a verb.

Examples:

a. Achan hid the accursed thing.

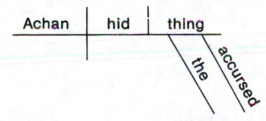

b. He had taken the Babylonian *garments* and shekels of *silver*.

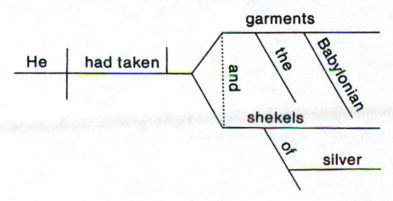

EXERCISE 7

Diagram the following sentences.

1. Joshua placed the various tribes of Israel on trial.

2. What did he do?

3. Achan transgressed God's law.

4. Joshua sent messengers to Achan's tents.

5. Joshua and all Israel took Achan and his spoils to the valley of Achor.

B. *Indirect object.* An *indirect object* tells to whom or for whom something is done.

Example:
God gave *Joshua* directions.

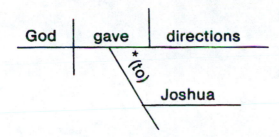

*Some grammarians omit the word *to* in the diagram.

EXERCISE 8

Diagram the following sentences.

1. Joshua gave Achan advice.

2. The Israelites gave him stern punishments.

3. They stoned Achan and burned him and his family with fire.

4. Then God promised Joshua the land of the king of Ai.

5. Joshua chose 30,000 men, mighty soldiers of valour.

C. *Predicate Nominative.* A *predicate nominative* or *subject complement* is a noun, pronoun, or adjective which follows a linking verb.

> **Examples:**
> a. Joshua was the leader.

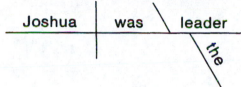

> b. The leader was he.

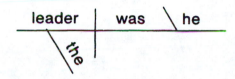

> c. He was strong.

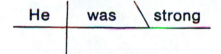

EXERCISE 9

Diagram the following sentences.

1. Joshua was crafty.

2. The army appeared frightened.

3. Twelve thousand men were killed.

4. A heap of stones became a memorial to this war.

5. The entire story is gruesome to us.

D. *Objective Complement.* An *objective complement* is a noun or adjective that completes the predicate and tells something about the direct object.

Example:
Thou shalt call His name Jesus.

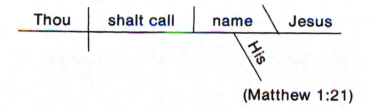

(Matthew 1:21)

EXERCISE 10

Diagram the following sentences.

1. They named the place The Valley of Achor.

2. The enemies of the Israelites called themselves servants.

3. That day Joshua made them hewers of wood.

4. These wars made people afraid.

5. God had appointed Joshua the leader.

IV. Verbals
A. *Participles.* A *participle* is a verb form used as an adjective.

Example:
The Hivites, *pretending friendship*, tricked Joshua.

EXERCISE 11

Diagram the following sentences.

1. Seeking safety, they told lies.

2. Hearing about your victories, we travelled from a far country.

3. The elders and Joshua, wanting peace, made an agreement with the enemies.

4. Other kings, fearing God's wrath, joined forces together.

5. Fleeing from the Israelites, the enemy was slaughtered.

B. *Infinitives.* An *infinitive* is a verb preceded by *to*. The infinitive phrase and its modifiers may be used as a noun, adjecive, or adverb.

Examples:

a. The Lord caused great stones *to be cast upon them.* (Infinitive phrase used as an adjective.)

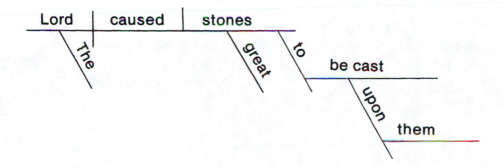

b. The sun hasted not *to go down about a whole day.* (Infinitive phrase used as an adverb.)

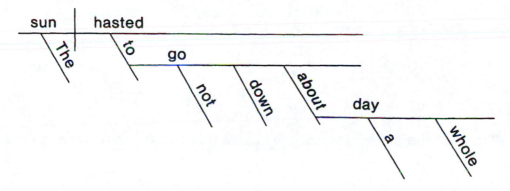

c. *To believe God* is *to live victoriously.* (Infinitive phrase used as a noun – a subject and a predicate noun.)

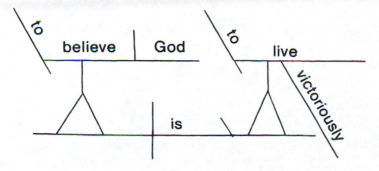

29

EXERCISE 12

Diagram the following sentences.

1. The five enemy kings tried to seek refuge in caves.

2. Joshua rolled stones upon the mouth of the cave to keep them.

3. The Lord continued to deliver Joshua and his men.

4. With God's help Joshua was able to defeat all the surrounding enemies.

5. To obey God is wise.

C. *Gerunds.* A *gerund* is a verb form used as a noun.

Examples:
a. *Waging war against the evil ones* was Joshua's duty. (Gerund used as a subject.)

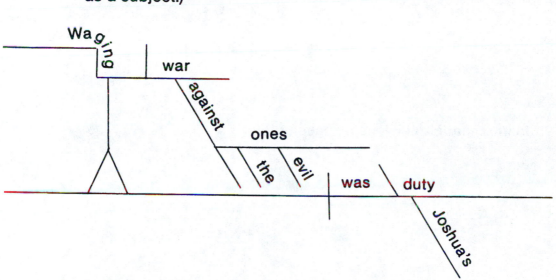

b. Joshua was responsible *for dividing the lands among the tribes.* (Gerund used as object of a preposition.)

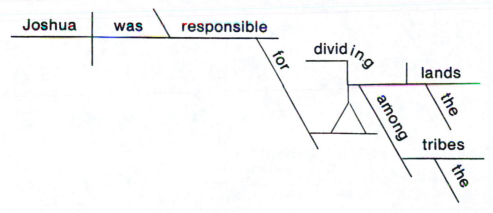

c. Joshua obeyed *God's leading.* (Gerund used as direct object.)

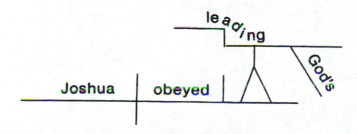

EXERCISE 13

Diagram the following sentences.

1. Setting up a tabernacle was another duty of the Israelites.

2. Joshua made decisions by casting lots.

3. God will do the fighting for you.

4. Chasing thousands is His delight.

5. Submit to God's leading.

V. Compound Sentences

Example:

Now Joshua was old and stricken in years, and the Lord spoke to him.

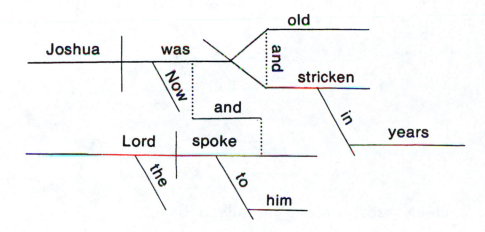

Diagram the following sentences.

1. There remains much land to be divided, and you must do it.

2. No land was given to the tribe of Levi, but they received a special inheritance.

3. Joshua blessed Caleb, and gave him Hebron.

4. Fear the Lord and serve Him in sincerity.

5. Take heed unto yourselves; love the Lord your God.

VI. Complex sentences
A. Noun Clause

Examples:
a. You have seen what God did for Israel. (Noun clause used as a direct object.)

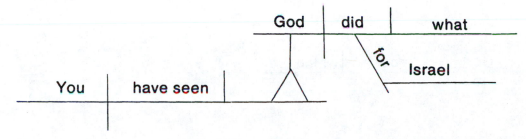

b. Whoever trusts God is wise. (Noun clause used as a subject)

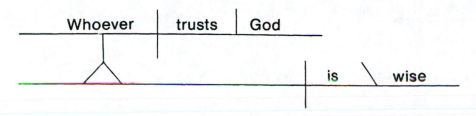

B. Adjective Clause

Examples:
a. The Lord is he that has fought for you.

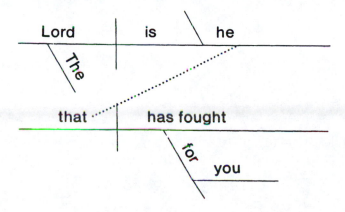

b. Nothing has failed of the good things which God spake concerning you.

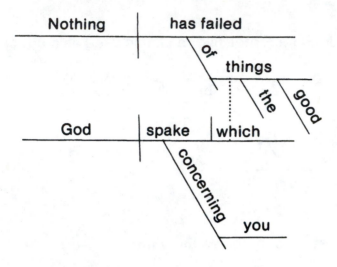

C. Adverb Clause
   Example:

You shall possess the land as God promised.

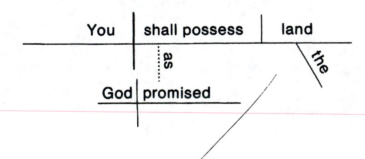

EXERCISE 15

Diagram the following sentences.

1. When you transgress the covenant of the Lord, He is not pleased.

2. God bestows blessings on those who obey Him.

3. Choose you this day whom you will serve.

4. As for me and my house, we will serve the Lord.

5. If you forsake the Lord, He will consume you.

EXPLORING TRUTHS

The material used in the diagrams is drawn from the book of *Joshua*.
Read *Joshua* and find a theme for the book.
What evidence did you find to justify your choice?
Is the theme a truth which is applicable in today's society?

ANSWERS

EXERCISE   1

1. —— Jesus | lives. ——

2. —— Joshua | led. ——

3. —— People | were praying. ——

4. —— They | yielded. ——

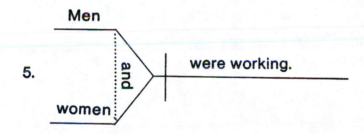

5. Men
    and
    women | were working.

EXERCISE 2

1.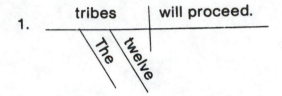
tribes | will proceed.
The twelve

2.
city | fell.
The fortified

3.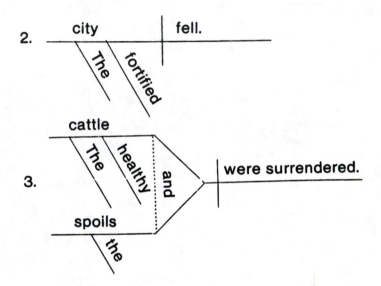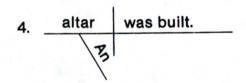
cattle
The healthy
and | were surrendered.
spoils
the

4.
altar | was built.
An

5.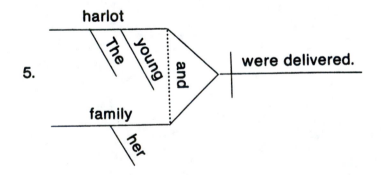
harlot
The young
and | were delivered.
family
her

40

EXERCISE 3

1.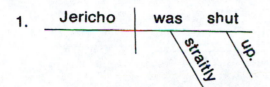

Jericho | was shut
straitly up.

2.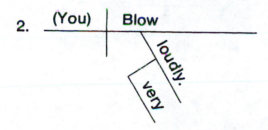

(You) | Blow
very loudly.

3.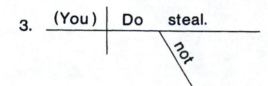

(You) | Do steal.
not

4.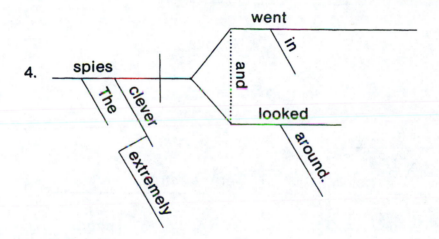

spies
The clever
extremely

went
in
and
looked
around.

5.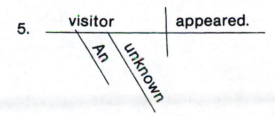

visitor | appeared.
An unknown

41

EXERCISE 4

1.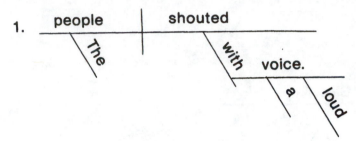
The people shouted with a loud voice.

2.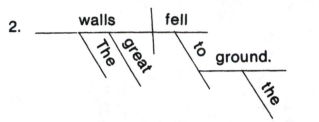
The great walls fell to the ground.

3.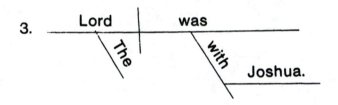
The Lord was with Joshua.

4.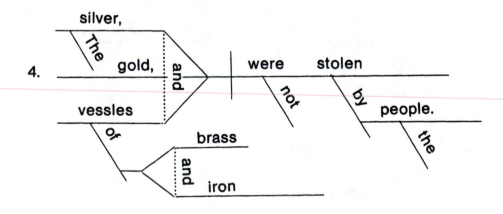
The silver, gold, and vessels of brass and iron were not stolen by the people.

5.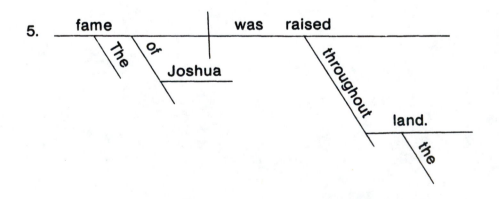
The fame of Joshua was raised throughout the land.

EXERCISE 5

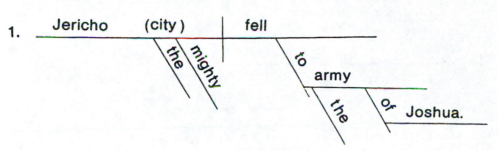

1. Jericho (city) | fell | to army | the | of Joshua.
   the / mighty

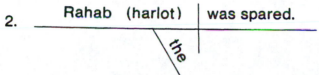

2. Rahab (harlot) | was spared.
   the

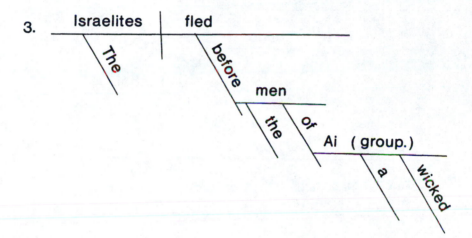

3. Israelites | fled | before men | the | of Ai (group.) | a | wicked
   The

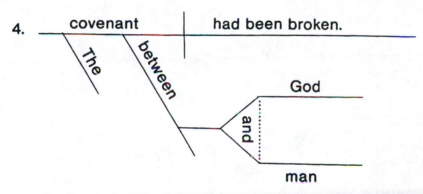

4. covenant | had been broken.
   The | between | God | and | man

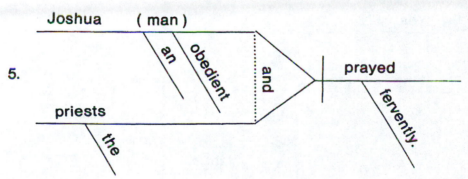

5. Joshua (man) | an obedient | and | prayed fervently.
   priests | the

EXERCISE 6

1.

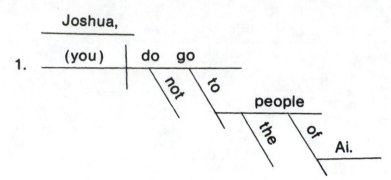

2.

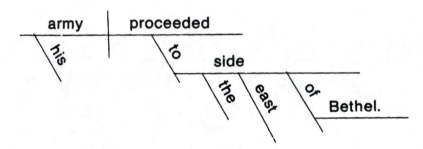

3.

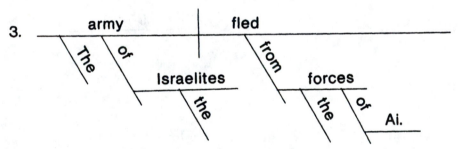

4.

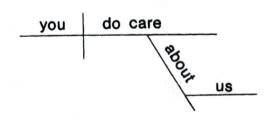

5.

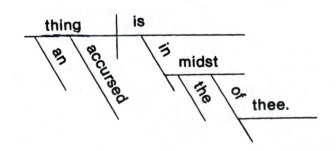

1.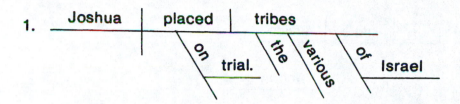

2.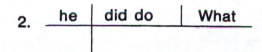

3.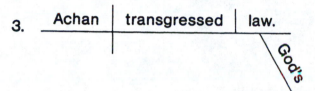

4.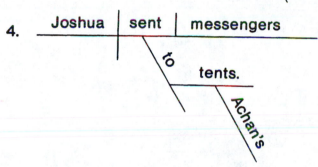

5.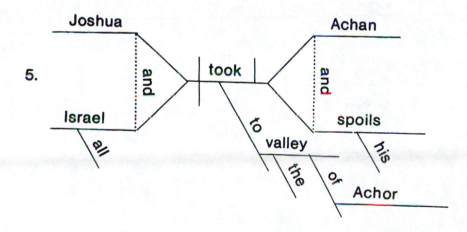

EXERCISE 8

1.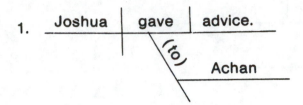

Joshua | gave | advice.
(to) Achan

2.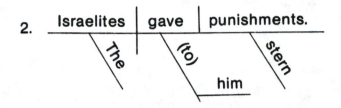

Israelites | gave | punishments.
The / (to) him \ stern

3.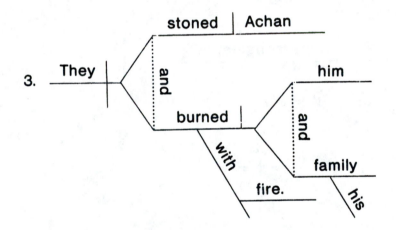

They | stoned | Achan
and
burned | him
and
with family
fire. his

4.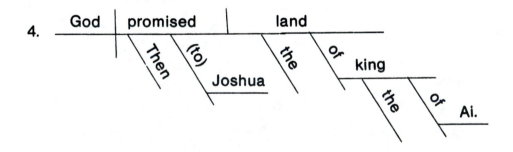

God | promised | land
Then / (to) Joshua / the / of king
the of Ai.

5.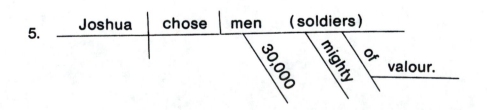

Joshua | chose | men (soldiers)
30,000 mighty of valour.

EXERCISE 9

1. Joshua | was \ crafty.

2.  army | appeared \ frightened.
   The

3. 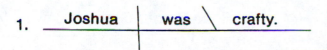 men | were killed.
   Twelve thousand

4. 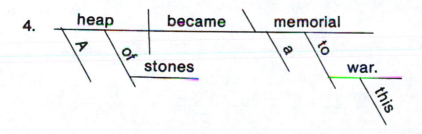 heap | became \ memorial
   A   of stones   a \ to
   war.
   this

5. 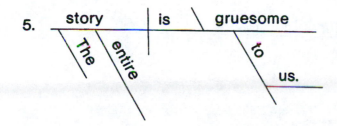 story | is \ gruesome
   The entire   to
   us.

47

1.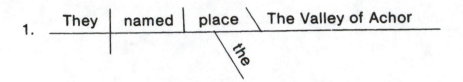

2.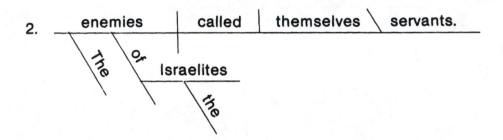

3.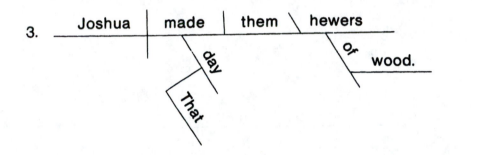

4.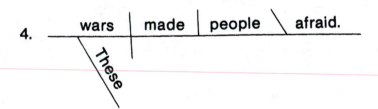

5.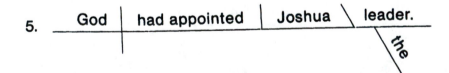

EXERCISE 11

1. they | told | lies.
   Seeking | safety

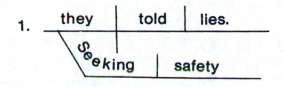

2. we | travelled
   Hearing | from country.
   about | victories | a | far | your

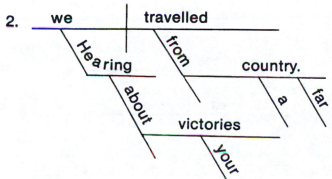

3. elders
   The and
   Joshua | made | agreement
   an | with | enemies. the
   wanting | peace

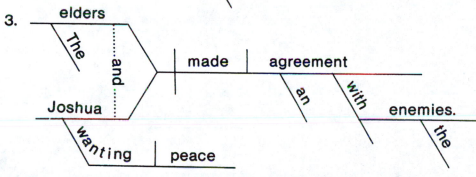

4. kings | joined | forces
   Other | fearing | wrath | together.
   God's

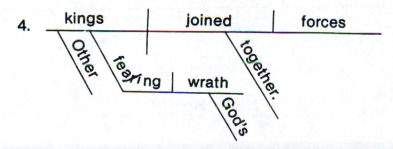

5. enemy | was slaughtered.
   the Fleeing
   from | Israelites | the

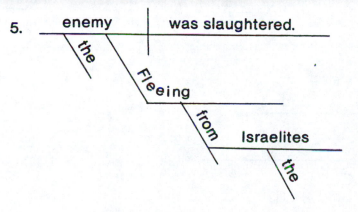

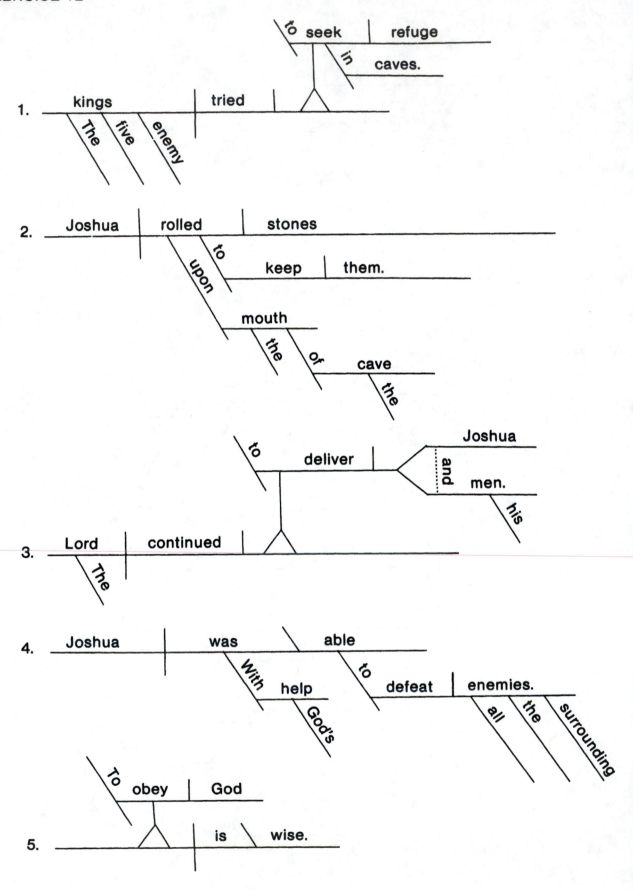

1.

2.

3.

4.

5.

1.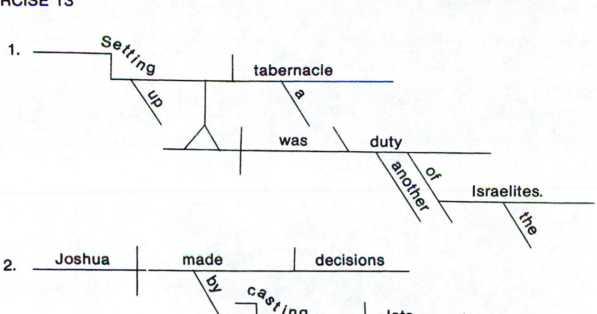

2.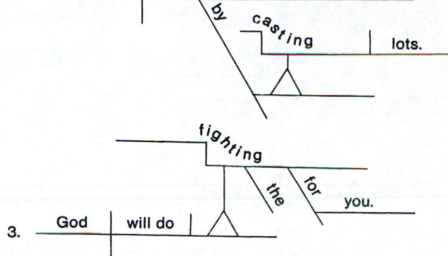

3.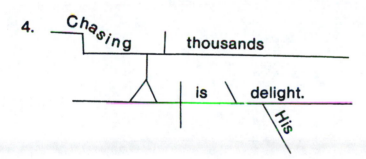

4.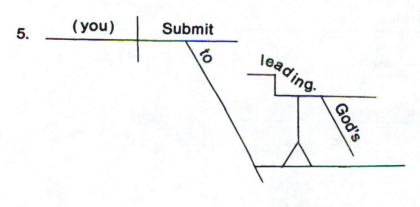

5.

EXERCISE 14

1.
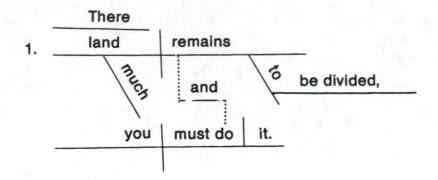

2.
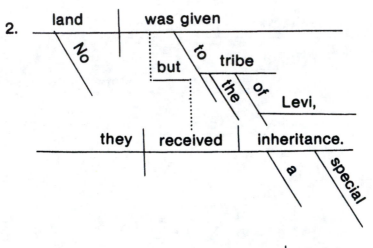

3.
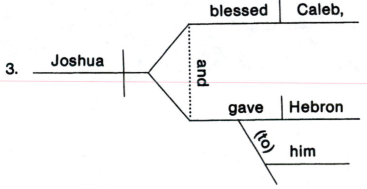

4.
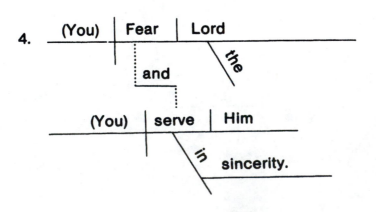

5.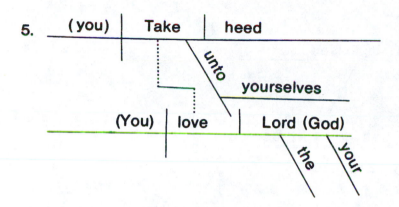

1.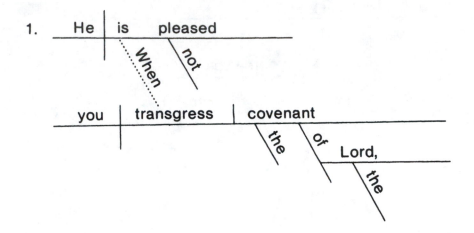

2.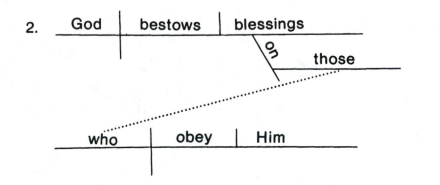

3.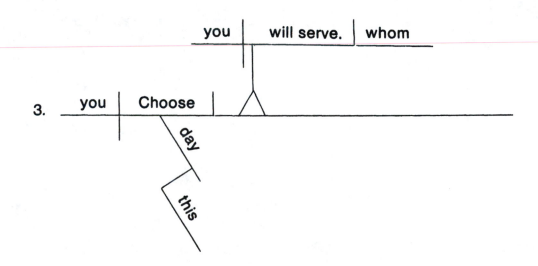

4.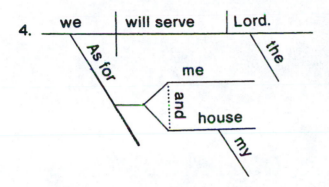

5.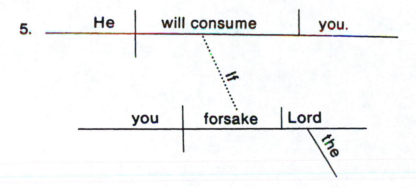

400
E167L

121557

Printed in the United States
15618LVS00001B/267-318

3 4711 00200 3087

9 780899 576022